WI-FI

CONNECTING US ONLINE

EMMETT MARTIN

Gareth Stevens
PUBLISHING

Please visit our website, www.garethstevens.com.
For a free color catalog of all our high-quality books,
call toll free 1-800-542-2595 or fax 1-877-542-2596.

Portions of this work were originally authored by A. S. Gintzler and published as *How Wi-Fi Works*. All new material in this edition authored by Emmett Martin.

Cataloging-in-Publication Data
Names: Martin, Emmett.
Title: Wi-Fi: Connecting us online / Emmett Martin.
Description: New York : Gareth Stevens, 2023. | Series: STEM is Everywhere| Includes glossary and index.
Identifiers: ISBN 9781538283677 (pbk.) | ISBN 9781538283691 (library bound) | ISBN 9781538283707 (ebook)
Subjects: LCSH: Electromagnetic energy –Juvenile literature. | Internet –Juvenile literature. | Wifi LANs –Juvenile literature.
Classification: LCC TK5103.4885 M37 2023 | DDC 004.6–dc23

Published in 2023 by
Gareth Stevens Publishing
2544 Clinton Street
Buffalo, NY 14224

Copyright © 2023 Gareth Stevens Publishing

Designer: Tanya Dellaccio
Editor: Therese Shea

Photo credits: Series Art Supphachai Salaeman/Shutterstock.com; cover Dmytro Zinkevych/Shutterstock.com; p; 5 HappyTime19/Shutterstock.com; p. 6 Trong Nguyen/Shutterstock.com; p. 7 Sutiwat Jutiamornloes/Shutterstock.com; p. 9 (top) Gorodenkoff/Shutterstock.com; p; 9 (bottom) https://upload.wikimedia.org/wikipedia/commons/d/dd/Vic_Hayes_75.jpg; p. 11 brgfx/Shutterstock.com; p. 13 (top) myboys.me/Shutterstock.com; p. 13 (bottm) petrroudny43/Shutterstock.com; p. 15 (bottom) Norman Chan/Shutterstock.com; p 15 (top) iunewind/Shutterstock.com; p. 17 (top) Prapat Aowsakorn/Shutterstock.com; p. 17 (bottom) aslysun/Shutterstock.com; p. 19 Prostock-studio/Shutterstock.com; p. 21 (bottom) Randall Vermillion/Shutterstock.com; p. 21 (top) FamVeld/Shutterstock.com; p. 23 Peter Togel/Shutterstock.com; p. 25 (bottom) Wi_Stock/Shutterstock.com; p. 25 (top) Camilo Concha/Shutterstock.com; p. 27 Mino Surkala/Shutterstck.com.

CPSIA compliance information: Batch #CWGS23: For further information contact Gareth Stevems Publishing at 1-800-398-2504.

Find us on

CONTENTS

Words in the glossary appear in **bold** type
the first time they are used in the text.

WHY WIRELESS?

Wi-Fi is a way to connect to the internet without using wires. Wi-Fi carries information, or data, to and from our computers, video game systems, tablets, smartphones, and other devices.

Why do you need Wi-Fi? It lets you move freely around with your device. You can sit in your favorite chair, lie by the pool, take a walk, or hang out at the park and still stay connected to the internet. Without Wi-Fi, you'd be stuck at a desk whenever you wanted to do your favorite online activities—or have to stay connected through a very long cable!

WI-FI LETS YOU GET ONLINE WITHOUT THE USE OF WIRES.

WHAT'S IN A NAME?

THE TERM "WI-FI" SOUNDS LIKE IT SHOULD BE SHORT FOR SOMETHING, BUT IT DOESN'T STAND FOR ANYTHING. AN ORGANIZATION CALLED THE WI-FI ALLIANCE AND A MARKETING COMPANY DECIDED ON THE NAME FOR THIS TECHNOLOGY. THEY THOUGHT IT WOULD BE EASY TO SAY AND REMEMBER, AND THAT IT WAS BETTER THAN THE ACTUAL NAME—IEEE 802.11.

BEFORE WIRELESS

At home, a modem usually provides the link to the internet. The modem is a small box that connects to an internet service provider's outside equipment, or gear, which is often a cable. Modems bring the internet into people's homes.

WHAT DO YOU DO ONLINE?

WI-FI MAKES IT SIMPLE TO DO YOUR FAVORITE INTERNET ACTIVITIES: SENDING AND RECEIVING MESSAGES AND VIDEOS, PLAYING ONLINE GAMES, WATCHING MOVIES AND TV SHOWS, AND MORE. YOU PROBABLY USE IT TO DO YOUR HOMEWORK TOO! WITHOUT WI-FI, YOU WOULD NEED TO HAVE YOUR SMART DEVICE PHYSICALLY CONNECTED TO THE INTERNET WITH A CABLE.

Before Wi-Fi, a device needed to be plugged into the modem to **access** the internet. That meant a computer could only be moved as far as a cable connecting them allowed. Even laptops, though easy to move around, had to be connected to the modem to access the internet. People wanted to move. Wi-Fi technology was the answer.

THE INVENTION OF WI-FI

Like most technology that has to do with computers, Wi-Fi wasn't invented by just one person. Instead, teams of scientists and engineers **developed** it. An Australian organization called the Commonwealth Scientific and Industrial Research Organisation (CSIRO), headed by Dr. John O'Sullivan, patented their wireless local area network (LAN) in the 1990s. But many scientists had been working on wireless networks before this.

In 1997, the Institute of Electrical and Electronics Engineers (IEEE) approved the first wireless standard, which is a set of rules and services that state how wireless networks should work. This standard—called IEEE 802.11—helped wireless devices from different companies work together.

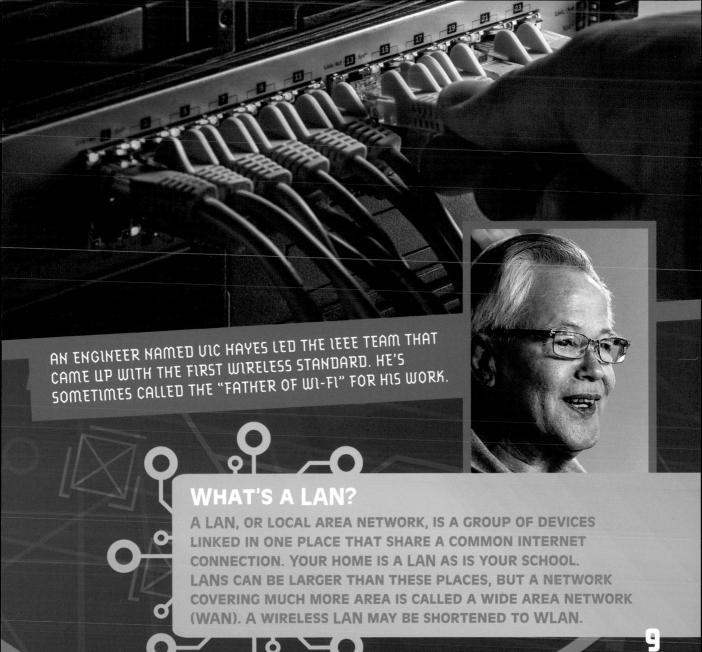

AN ENGINEER NAMED VIC HAYES LED THE IEEE TEAM THAT CAME UP WITH THE FIRST WIRELESS STANDARD. HE'S SOMETIMES CALLED THE "FATHER OF WI-FI" FOR HIS WORK.

WHAT'S A LAN?

A LAN, OR LOCAL AREA NETWORK, IS A GROUP OF DEVICES LINKED IN ONE PLACE THAT SHARE A COMMON INTERNET CONNECTION. YOUR HOME IS A LAN AS IS YOUR SCHOOL. LANS CAN BE LARGER THAN THESE PLACES, BUT A NETWORK COVERING MUCH MORE AREA IS CALLED A WIDE AREA NETWORK (WAN). A WIRELESS LAN MAY BE SHORTENED TO WLAN.

WHAT WAVES?

So if Wi-Fi doesn't use wires, what is it using to transmit data? Radio waves! Radio waves are waves of **electromagnetic** energy. They have certain features that make them good for communication. They travel through the air, don't harm people's bodies, and can be reflected in different directions.

MORE KINDS OF ENERGY

YOU'RE LIKELY FAMILIAR WITH OTHER KINDS OF ELECTROMAGNETIC WAVES. FOR EXAMPLE, ALL THE COLORS THAT WE KNOW AS VISIBLE LIGHT ARE ELECTROMAGNETIC WAVES. X-RAYS ARE USED IN MEDICINE. THEY CAN TRAVEL THROUGH THE SOFT PARTS OF OUR BODIES TO CREATE IMAGES OF OUR BONES. MICROWAVES THAT HEAT OUR FOOD ARE A KIND OF RADIO WAVE.

ELECTROMAGNETIC SPECTRUM

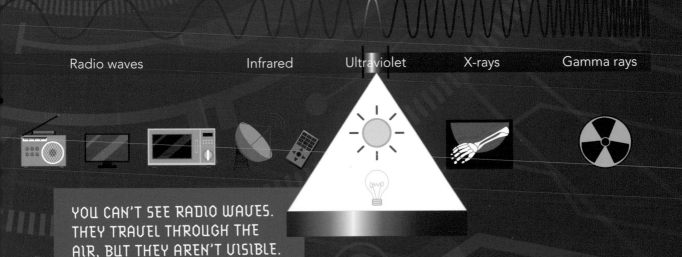

Radio waves   Infrared   Ultraviolet   X-rays   Gamma rays

YOU CAN'T SEE RADIO WAVES. THEY TRAVEL THROUGH THE AIR, BUT THEY AREN'T VISIBLE.

Have you ever thrown a rock into a lake? Did you see the circles ripple out? One wave follows another. This image can help you understand electromagnetic waves. The distance between a point on one wave to the same point on the next is called the wavelength. Radio waves have the longest wavelength of the different kinds of electromagnetic waves.

Radio waves have the lowest frequency of electromagnetic waves. The frequency is how many waves pass through a point each second. Still, radio waves can have different frequencies. Some have higher frequencies, or more waves per second. Others have lower frequencies, or fewer. Scientists figured out that high-frequency radio waves can carry more data than low-frequency waves. Wi-Fi uses high-frequency radio waves.

HIGH AND LOW

HIGH-FREQUENCY RADIO WAVES ARE ALSO USED FOR CELL PHONE CALLS, FM RADIO, AND GPS (GLOBAL POSITIONING SYSTEM). LOW-FREQUENCY WAVES, THOUGH THEY CARRY LESS DATA, ARE USEFUL TOO. THE LOWEST FREQUENCIES CAN GO LONG DISTANCES AND PASS THROUGH ROCK AND OTHER HARD SURFACES, FOR EXAMPLE SENDING COMMUNICATIONS TO PEOPLE IN CAVES AND MINES.

Frequency

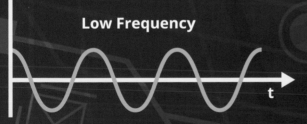

Low Frequency

t

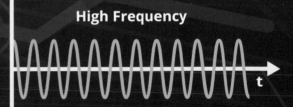

High Frequency

t

All devices that work using radio waves, such as radios, smartphones, TVs, and computers, need a transmitter to send out radio waves and a receiver to collect them. These may be built into a device's antenna or antennae.

WI-FI AT WORK

For Wi-Fi to work in your devices at home, they each need to have a wireless adapter. These are usually built into devices. You also need a **router**. When you use Wi-Fi, your device uses electricity to **translate** data into radio waves and sends them out into the air. The antennae of the router pick up the radio waves, sometimes called radio signals.

The router is likely connected to a modem. The modem transmits the data out of your house and onto the internet. Some devices act as both a modem and router in one.

BINARY CODE

WHAT DOES A COMPUTER'S DATA LOOK LIKE? IT DOESN'T LOOK LIKE PICTURES OR WORDS. ALL DATA IN COMPUTERS AND SIMILAR DEVICES IS IN BINARY CODE, WHICH IS A PATTERN OF 1s AND 0s. YOU COULD THINK OF IT AS A LANGUAGE THAT COMPUTERS CAN READ. THESE 1s AND 0s ARE WHAT'S TRANSLATED INTO RADIO WAVES.

WHILE THE ROUTER PROVIDES WIRELESS INTERNET, THE MODEM TO WHICH IT IS LINKED NEEDS TO BE CONNECTED BY WIRES, OR A CABLE, TO AN OUTSIDE INTERNET CONNECTION.

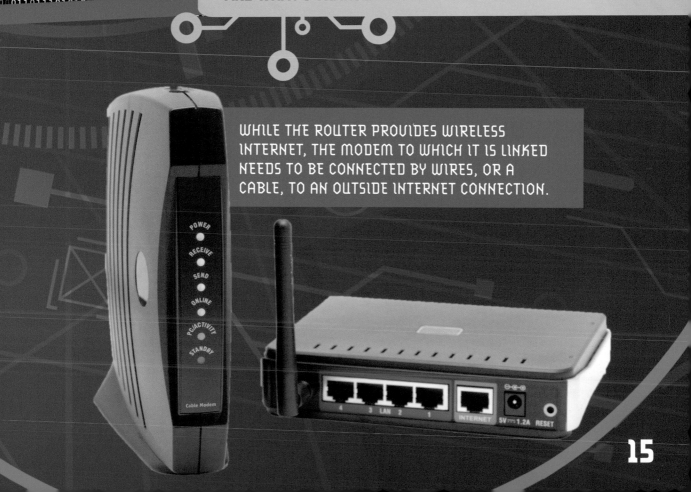

Information from outside internet networks comes back to your Wi-Fi device in the reverse way. It comes to your neighborhood using your internet service provider's equipment. It connects to your house through your modem and goes to your router. The data is translated into radio waves by your router and sent out through the router antennae. If your device is in range, it will receive the data.

ESSENTIAL ELECTRICITY

IN WI-FI, DATA IN THE FORM OF ELECTRICAL SIGNALS IS TRANSLATED INTO RADIO WAVES AND THEN BACK INTO ELECTRICAL SIGNALS. THIS MEANS THAT ELECTRICITY IS NEEDED TO MAKE WI-FI WORK. AN UNPLUGGED ROUTER OR MODEM OR A POWER OUTAGE CAN MEAN YOUR WI-FI MAY GO OUT, CAUSING YOU TO LOSE YOUR CONNECTION.

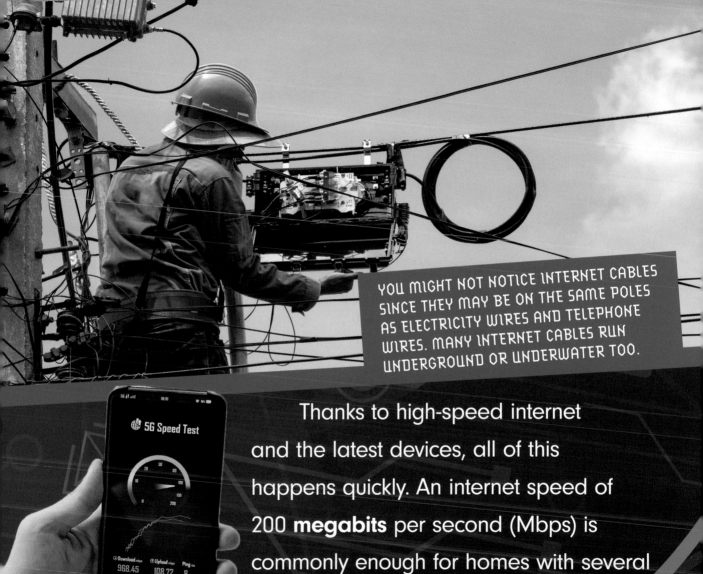

YOU MIGHT NOT NOTICE INTERNET CABLES SINCE THEY MAY BE ON THE SAME POLES AS ELECTRICITY WIRES AND TELEPHONE WIRES. MANY INTERNET CABLES RUN UNDERGROUND OR UNDERWATER TOO.

Thanks to high-speed internet and the latest devices, all of this happens quickly. An internet speed of 200 **megabits** per second (Mbps) is commonly enough for homes with several people using Wi-Fi at the same time.

GAME ON

Imagine you're playing a game on your tablet. Many game **platforms** such as Roblox are cloud-based. That means the game you're playing is on a server accessed through the internet. It's not on your device. You need to be connected to the internet while you're playing it. You likely won't connect your tablet to your modem with a cable. You'll use Wi-Fi.

Everything you do within your game is data that is sent by your tablet over Wi-Fi to the internet. And every new scene or choice the game shows you is data being sent back through the internet that is transferred by Wi-Fi to your tablet.

PLAYING ONLINE GAMES REQUIRES A LOT OF DATA FLOWING VERY QUICKLY THROUGH YOUR WI-FI CONNECTION.

ALL IN THE CLOUD

THE CLOUD IS THE NAME FOR THE COLLECTION OF DATA THAT'S STORED IN POWERFUL COMPUTERS CALLED SERVERS, WHICH CAN BE ACCESSED THROUGH THE INTERNET. CLOUD STORAGE MEANS LESS DATA NEEDS TO BE SAVED ON PEOPLE'S HOME DEVICES. YOU USE THE CLOUD EVERY TIME YOU STREAM MOVIES OR MUSIC, OR PLAY CLOUD-BASED GAMES.

HOT SPOT!

Lots of people access Wi-Fi on their home network, but Wi-Fi is also available in many public places. Any internet network that people can access is called a hot spot or a hub. Public libraries, coffee shops, restaurants, hotels, and other places often offer people hot spots to connect to the internet. Sometimes businesses charge customers a fee to use it, though.

Nearly all U.S. schools have an internet connection, though not all offer Wi-Fi yet. But about 12 million students in the United States don't have access to high-speed internet at home, which can affect their ability to do some kinds of schoolwork.

INTERNET AND EDUCATION

DURING THE COVID-19 PANDEMIC, INTERNET ACCESS BECAME A MAJOR CONCERN IN EDUCATION. STUDENTS HAD TO STAY HOME FROM SCHOOL. THEY HAD TO USE THE INTERNET TO CONNECT WITH TEACHERS AND CONTINUE LEARNING. THOSE STUDENTS WHO DIDN'T HAVE A GOOD INTERNET CONNECTION OR WHO DIDN'T HAVE COMPUTERS OR TABLETS COULDN'T KEEP UP WITH THEIR STUDIES.

THE SYMBOL, OR IMAGE, FOR WI-FI SHOWS LINES CURVED LIKE WAVES.

HOW FAR?

Wi-Fi signals for a home network from the average router can travel up to 150 feet (46 m) indoors and up to 300 feet (91 m) outdoors. Thick walls and other **obstacles** can limit signal strength, however. Older equipment and the number of people using your network can also affect signal strength.

REACHING OUT

CELL PHONES USE RADIO WAVES FOR SENDING AND RECEIVING CALLS. SOME PHONES REACH SIGNALS UP TO 45 MILES (72 KM) AWAY. THAT'S SO MUCH FARTHER THAN WI-FI! BUT WI-FI'S DATA TRANSMISSION RATE IS MORE THAN 1,000 TIMES HIGHER THAN WHEN IT WAS FIRST INTRODUCED. ENGINEERS ARE WORKING ON WAYS TO MAKE ITS RANGE BETTER TOO.

A WI-FI RANGE EXTENDER IS PLACED BETWEEN A ROUTER AND THE AREA NOT RECEIVING WI-FI. THE EXTENDER RECEIVES THE SIGNALS AND PUSHES THEM FARTHER.

If your Wi-Fi at home doesn't seem to be working well, you can try to fix it by making sure the router is placed in a central location. You can also buy a device called a range extender to boost the signal so it reaches all parts of your home.

WI-FI SAFETY

Public Wi-Fi can be really handy since anyone can use it. It has drawbacks, though. You shouldn't do anything on public Wi-Fi that could show others on the network private information, such as usernames and passwords. People called hackers can spy on others through public Wi-Fi. They can collect information that can help them get into email and bank accounts. They may sell data to others or try to use it for their own gain.

It's a good idea to protect yourself by using different passwords for different websites. Also, sites with a lock symbol next to the website name are usually safer to use that sites without it.

PRIVATE WI-FI HOT SPOTS SHOULD REQUIRE A USERNAME AND PASSWORD SO THAT ONLY PEOPLE TRUSTED WITH THIS INFORMATION CAN ACCESS THE NETWORK.

PORTABLE HOT SPOT

MANY SMARTPHONES AND TABLETS PRODUCED TODAY OFFER THE ABILITY TO TURN THE DEVICE INTO ITS OWN HOT SPOT. HOWEVER, THIS USUALLY USES UP DATA (IF YOU'RE ONLY ALLOWED TO USE A CERTAIN AMOUNT BY YOUR SERVICE PROVIDER). IT ALSO USES UP BATTERY POWER. MOBILE HOT SPOT DEVICES ARE ALSO AVAILABLE FOR A FEE.

FREQUENCY FACTS

Routers use frequency bands, or ranges of radio wave frequencies, to send data. Routers once used just two bands: 2.4 gigahertz (GHz) and 5 GHz. The 2.4 GHz band offered better range, and the 5 GHz band offered faster speeds. In 2020, the 6 GHz band was opened for use, which meant even faster and more stable Wi-Fi connections.

Each band has a number of channels through which your data travels. A router will usually choose the band and channels for you. But you can change them if you think the Wi-Fi isn't working well for you.

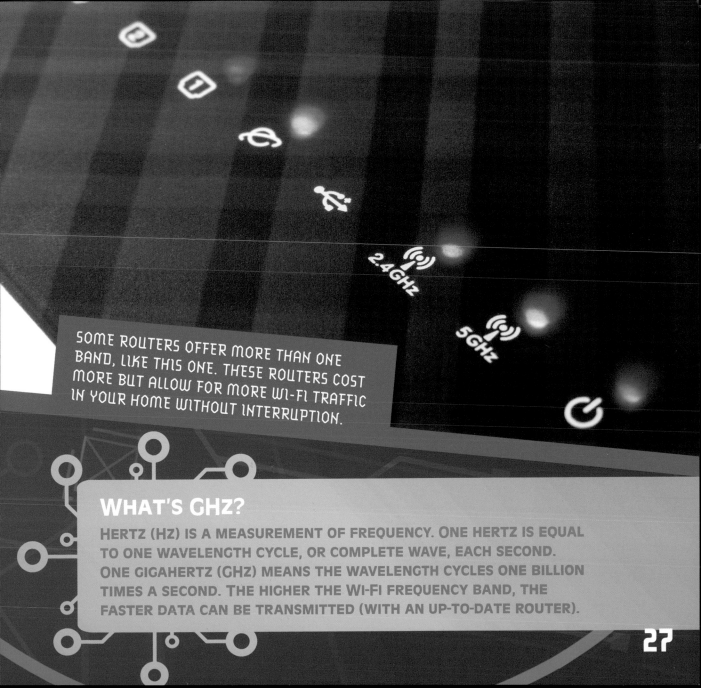

SOME ROUTERS OFFER MORE THAN ONE BAND, LIKE THIS ONE. THESE ROUTERS COST MORE BUT ALLOW FOR MORE WI-FI TRAFFIC IN YOUR HOME WITHOUT INTERRUPTION.

WHAT'S GHZ?

HERTZ (HZ) IS A MEASUREMENT OF FREQUENCY. ONE HERTZ IS EQUAL TO ONE WAVELENGTH CYCLE, OR COMPLETE WAVE, EACH SECOND. ONE GIGAHERTZ (GHZ) MEANS THE WAVELENGTH CYCLES ONE BILLION TIMES A SECOND. THE HIGHER THE WI-FI FREQUENCY BAND, THE FASTER DATA CAN BE TRANSMITTED (WITH AN UP-TO-DATE ROUTER).

FARTHER AND FASTER

The IEEE updates Wi-Fi standards as technology improves. The standards once had names like 802.11n and 802.11ac. Now they're called Wi-Fi 1, 2, 3, 4, 5, and so on. Wi-Fi 6 was adopted in 2019, and Wi-Fi 7 is expected by 2024. It should offer longer range, more stable connections, and faster data rates. Make sure your router at home is set up to work with the latest standard for the best Wi-Fi connection.

Can you picture going back to a time before Wi-Fi? It's hard to imagine, isn't it? Thanks to this amazing technology, we're headed for a wireless world. Wi-Fi will continue to keep us connected.

A TIMELINE OF WI-FI

1800s — HEINRICH HERTZ PROVES RADIO WAVES EXIST.

1906 — REGINALD FESSENDEN BECOMES THE FIRST PERSON TO TRANSMIT HIS VOICE WIRELESSLY, USING RADIO WAVES.

1971 — AN EARLY KIND OF WIRELESS NETWORK USING RADIO WAVES CONNECTS ISLANDS OF HAWAII.

1974 — THE FIRST ROUTERS ARE USED BY THE XEROX COMPANY.

1983 — A STANDARD WAY FOR COMPUTERS TO TALK TO EACH OTHER IS INTRODUCED, ALLOWING FOR THE MODERN INTERNET.

1991 — THE FIRST WEB PAGE GOES LIVE ON THE INTERNET.

1996 — JOHN O'SULLIVAN AND CSIRO PATENT A WIRELESS NETWORK.

1997 — VIC HAYES AND THE IEEE CREATE THE FIRST WIRELESS STANDARD.

1999 — THE TERM WI-FI IS ADOPTED FOR THE FIRST WIRELESS STANDARD.

2004 — DEVICES THAT CAN USE WI-FI, SUCH AS CELL PHONES, BEGIN TO BE SOLD.

2011 — MORE THAN 1 MILLION WI-FI HOT SPOTS ARE RECORDED AROUND THE WORLD.

2019 — WI-FI 6 IS INTRODUCED AS THE NEWEST STANDARD.

2020 — THE U.S. FEDERAL COMMUNICATIONS COMMISSION VOTED TO ALLOW THE USE OF THE 6 GHZ FREQUENCY BAND, PAVING THE WAY FOR FASTER WI-FI SPEEDS.

HERE ARE SOME OF THE MAJOR MOMENTS IN WIRELESS TECHNOLOGY.

GLOSSARY

access: To have the right or ability to use something.

develop: To put effort into producing something over time.

electromagnetic: Relating to the magnetic field that's produced by a current of electricity.

GPS: Stands for Global Positioning System. A system that uses satellite signals to locate places on Earth.

megabit: A unit of measurement for data size, often having to do with data transfer. (A bit is the smallest unit of computer data. A megabit is about the size of 1 million bits.)

obstacle: Something that blocks a path.

pandemic: An illness that is widely spread over several nations or the world.

physically: In a way that can be seen or touched.

platform: A program, or set of data, that oversees the way a computer works and runs other programs.

router: A machine designed to send data from one place to another within a computer network or between computer networks.

stream: To send or receive a media file in a stream of data that a receiving computer processes before the whole file is sent and does not store in its memory.

technology: A machine, piece of equipment, or method created by science, engineering, and other industries as a tool or as a way to solve a problem.

translate: To tell what words or text in one language mean in another.

FOR MORE INFORMATION

BOOKS

Eboch, M.M. *How Does Wi-Fi Work?* North Mankato, MN: Capstone Press, 2021.

Garstecki, Julia. *Radio Waves.* North Mankato, MN: Capstone, 2021.

Koestler-Grack, Rachel A. *Wireless Technology From Then to Now.* Mankato, MN: Amicus, 2020.

WEBSITES

How Wi-Fi Works
computer.howstuffworks.com/wireless-network.htm
Learn much more about what's going on in your home network and online.

Radio Waves, Microwaves, Infrared, and Visible light
www.bbc.co.uk/bitesize/guides/z9bw6yc/revision/4#
Find out how electricity creates radio waves.

Wi-Fi
kids.britannica.com/students/article/Wi-Fi/545141#
Check out more details about how this technology developed.

INDEX